FRESH BREAD
&
FLOWING WATER

RESTORATION OF THE BREACH
WITHOUT BORDERS

West Palm Beach, Fl, 33407

RICARDO O.
HENRY

ISBN: 978-1-954755-54-3

Published by:
Restoration of the Breach without Borders
West Palm Beach, Florida 33407
restorativeauthor@gmail.com
Tele: (561) 388-2949

Cover Design aided by:
Leostone Morrison

Editor: Melisha Bartley Ankle

Formatting and Publishing done by:
Leostone Morrison

With love, thankfulness and prayers, I dedicate this book to:

My wife Tamara and sons Jordaan, Joshuua and, Juude. May the light of the word shine upon you in this generation and the generations to come a Psalm 1 legacy is your portion. Additionally, my captive audiences in the **Next Level Let's Climb WhatsApp Group, and Thursday Night Live Bible Study via YouTube and Facebook and the wider Restoration of the Breach Without Borders Ministry.**

My FreshBread: Henry Chronicles Podcast listeners, the original WhatsApp devotional ministry – Koinonia Mobile Ministry (circa 2012) via WhatsApp. My **For God's Glory Only Ministry** (YouTube) family of viewers and word-sharers and my local church family- Pastor Dewey and the **Land O'Lakes Church of God.**

My chief cheerleading Hebrews 12:1 front row **Marie, Keisha Lavare, Tamika** & Kir and the cheerie section CAJB, Jerome & Veon, Dale, Ms G., Elysia & Dave, Glen & Michelle, Ryan, Rodeisha, Alphanso, Judith & Ransford, Shero, Lillett & Faxton, Nicole, Annette, Ann-Marie. Melisha, Remone, DonnaM, AngellaT, Richie & Lorna, Sis Chris & Bro Dave, Marcia, Geron, Melissa, Ava, Ralston & Samantha, Mother J, Bishop & Lady Morris. Spence, Dwight & Marsha. H-GH;

The company of seekers, folk who want to know more of God, who cannot get enough.

My mom departed, Sis Henry. My other moms, Angella, Zena.

And to my Father the One God of the universe who made all things who sent Jesus and through the Holy Spirit draws us to Himself to have fellowship.

iv

ACKNOWLEDGEMENTS

Restoration of the Breach Without Borders Ministry Leadership Team; Leostone Morrison and Hillary Dunkley-Campbell, Melisha Bartley Ankle, RBWBM NLLC presenters and prayer partners thanks for the nudge and outright push along with the technical and administrative support needed to bring these pages to print.

The Next level Let's Climb WhatsApp Bible Study Group, Koinonia Mobile Ministry, George Town & West Bay New Testament Churches of God and the Land O'Lakes Church of God who sanctioned these and were listening longingly as the Holy Spirit downloaded in their hearing.

The Caribbean International Zoom Prayer Movement led by Bishop Ishmael Charles in which the download regarding Joseph and his valiant resistance against the spirits of pride and porneia took shape and was first shared.

Tamara, Joshuua and Juude, you sacrificed some of your time with me so I had the opportunity to reflect, write, pray, sing,brood and produce what has now become the forerunner of other works.. I pray that as you sacrificed, prayed, sang with and played for me that you will also write with me as we together tell the world that Jesus is mighty to save, deliver and set free from sin.

Special acknowledgement to those who asked, "where is the book sir?" There are also those who insisted, "It is time." Another even offered to be the editor at the time appointed. Thank you! Thank you, reader!

Thank God for GRACE!

FOREWORD

The Spirit of the Lord GOD is upon me;

because the LORD hath anointed me to preach good tidings unto the meek; he hath sent me to bind up the brokenhearted, to proclaim liberty to the captives, and the opening of the prison to them that are bound (Isaiah 60:1). This is the mission Jesus extended to us. This is the admonition seen throughout the New Testament as the Apostles, Paul and the other brethren brought the Light to all who would receive Him. Throughout these pages we see the Light of Life shining as we consider the posture of our heart while we wait.

An important theme throughout the devotional is that idea of the Word, Fresh Bread, watering our souls. Whether it is considering our company and the value they bring or remove from our lives or taking an alone stance, it is the word being at the center that nutrifies our spirit to take a righteous stand. Stand even when your stance is against the vulture, stand against social injustice and norms that threaten the moral fabric of society and our faith. Stand when challenged by the devil to sin; and stand when life weighs on you to faint because of the frailty of your humanity.

The great hymn written by Rev Ray Palmer echoes our intercession – My faith looks up to Thee Thou Lamb of Calvary, Savior divine. It is this precious Lamb of God who is presented in Fresh Bread and Flowing water for our desert places. As you read the pages consider each key point, and each prayer; then walk away with the word of encouragement as a keepsake. Shalom!

ENDORSEMENTS

"The reflection of thoughts that Bishop Ricardo Henry articulated in this book are essential and relevant.

Why? Because the reality that stares us in the face in these trying times is very terrifying. My endorsement and recommendation of these encouraging and essential thoughts are nuggets that bring hope to a fatigued mind. This devotional, inspiring, motivational and Spirit filled book is one that all should read and digest repeatedly."

- Bishop Eitel Morris,
Administrative Bishop, New
Testament Church of God,
Cayman Islands

* * * * * *

"Fresh Bread & Flowing Water" – AWESOME!

This devotional reached the very core of my being, as it caused me to reflect deeply. As a Minister of Religion, this book moved me with its practical and personal insights that calls us to trust and rely on God for our everyday connection. Indeed, this is fresh bread for the soul. I recommend getting a copy of this book to add to your daily quiet time sessions, also I further encourage you to get more than one copy to share with everyone you know.

-Nasel Ephraim Pastor,
Leader, Speaker, and
Author

＊ ＊ ＊ ＊ ＊ ＊

It is always a blessing when God's people are inspired to write and vocalize their thoughts on faith perspectives. Bishop Ricardo Henry is a gifted, anointed and talented servant of the Lord, who through his ministry will provide godly insights and wisdom to provoke, push and propel you into a dimension of spiritual understanding and purpose, that will elevate you to think and act accordingly. I wholeheartedly endorse him and his spiritual perspective in this amazing devotional.

-Bishop Ransford, Lead Pastor: Destiny Gospel Centre Markham, Ontario, Canada

TABLE OF CONTENTS

DAY 1

WHILE YOU ARE WAITING...

Job 1: 8-27

Waiting is inevitable but, based on choice, it can become the place of victory or defeat. Many victories are denied because individuals squander the opportunities that waiting has granted unto them. Therefore, great care must be exercised when waiting becomes necessary. Three ways to maximize the waiting period:

❖ Remain Faithful

Never allow the pain associated with waiting to derail you from the place of faithfulness. Hebrew 11:6 states, 'Without faith it is impossible to please God;' therefore, as you navigate the pains of waiting, pleasing God remains the

1

greatest priority. Regardless of the situation, pain is never an exemption card.

❖ Greater Level of Faithfulness

Satan and by extension the kingdom of darkness will always scrutinize and challenge your faithfulness to God. In Job chapter 1 Satan, in his bid to attack, told God that Job's faithfulness was connected to the blessings he received. Therefore, with God's permission, the devil killed his children and afflicted him with sickness, but Job continued to trust God. Although the wait seemed long and the recovery far reaching, he remained faithful to God. Like Job, waiting will expose the sincerity of your faithfulness; the longer the wait, the greater the faithfulness that will be required.

❖ Stay focused, do not become frustrated

2

You may feel like Cinderella without her magic shoes; the wait, the burdens of the journey, everything seems more difficult to carry. Frustration has taken over and the thought of failure is your forever friend but stay focused. Choose to keep your eyes on the prize. Refuse to become limited by what the natural eyes are seeing. Shift your perspective, look ahead, and place your focus on that which you await. Waiting becomes lighter when focus is fully aligned.

Prayer

Lord as I wait, help me to remain faithful to You. Let waiting be easy in Jesus' name. Amen

Be encouraged...

You Are Not Built to Break!

DAY 2

KING DAVID WAITED

1 Samuel 16

Whenever the Lord ushers you into a period of

waiting; be comforted, you are among the

greats. David, recognized by God as a man after

His heart and the greatest king of Israel, was no

stranger to waiting.

❖ Is there another?

Samuel, the prophet, went to Jesse's house to

anoint one of his sons to be the next king of

Israel but the father only allowed seven of the

eight to stand before the prophet. The brothers

were all positioned to be anointed but David, the

rejected son, was not even invited. However,

fortunately for him, God's rejection of his

brothers forced Samuel to ask the dreaded

4

question, 'is there another?' Subsequently, David, who was tending his father's sheep, was called, and anointed the next king of Israel.

❖ Anointed but not appointed

The narrative shifted from the expected; David was anointed but he had to wait fifteen years to ascend the throne. Therefore, be patient; anointing and appointment are separate and may manifest in stages.

❖ Serving amid the THREATS.

During his fifteen years' wait David had to serve the reigning King Saul. However, the wait was not smooth as the king sought to kill him on many occasions. Therefore, in his pursuit of survival, David had to quickly learn that the waiting period requires vigilance. The anointing does not negate being alert or threatened by the enemy. While you wait remain watchful or you will die.

Prayer

Father in the name of Jesus, as I wait and serve, help me to effectively navigate the arrows of death, sickness, and defeat. Amen

Be encouraged...

"Wait without the weight"

DAY 3

WAITING...WHAT WILL YOU DO?

Romans 12:1-2

Idle hands are seeds for destruction. Therefore, what will you do while waiting?

❖ **Single and waiting...**

The flesh is a bully and hates waiting. As a result, waiting can be challenging and is sometimes intensified by the state of being single. However, singleness is a gift and its purity must be treasured. Consequently, the pressure placed on singles to get married and satisfy the desires of the flesh should not be encouraged. While you wait let your mantra be Romans 12: 1-2(NIV).

"Therefore, I urge you, brothers, and sisters, in view of God's mercy, to offer your bodies as a living sacrifice, holy and pleasing to God—this is your true and proper worship. Do not conform to the pattern of this world, but be transformed by the renewing of your mind…'

❖ **Called but waiting**

A doctor's visit will require registration followed by a waiting period. After the initial wait, the patient is called to the triage area for preliminary checks and gathering of information but thereafter he or she is asked to wait again. However, while the wait drags on, the completed registration gives the assurance that the time spent is not in vain; the time will come when that person will be called to see the doctor.   In the same manner, after being called, life will sometimes require waiting but this should be done willingly for victory will soon call your name.

❖ Trained but waiting

The army consists of regular and specialist squads. While the regular will be seen often, the specialist is only called when needed; both groups are trained but the latter must wait to be summoned. You are not regular; you are a specialist. However, while you remain in reserve do not become super spiritual and miss what God is doing; listen for His directives. A trained soldier not only understands the wealth in waiting but he or she knows when and how to enter the field to collect the blessings.

Prayer

Lord, whether I am in the single, called, or trained mode, please teach me how to wait. Amen

Be encouraged...

You are not wasting away, you are waiting.

DAY 4

WHO IS GOING WITH YOU?

2 Kings 2

Partnership is an asset. Nevertheless, to avoid unnecessary pain, delays, and ultimate failures, said expensive decision must be taken with care.

❖ Divine Connections

While the disciples prayed and worshipped, Paul and Barnabas were selected by the Holy Spirit. "While they were worshiping the Lord and fasting, the Holy Spirit said, "Set apart for me Barnabas and Saul for the work to which I have called them" Acts 13:2. We must be keen to ensure that the persons on the journey are the ones with the divine connection.

11

❖ Stick-to-itiveness

In Daniel chapter 3, the Hebrew Boys demonstrated togetherness in faith and in the face of death; they did not quit or abandon each other when the negative consequences of staying true to their faith intensified. Have we truly evaluated with whom we have bonded? Is the bond maximized during pleasantries or is the strength of the togetherness realized in crisis? Do not make the error of committing to someone who is not truly devoted to you.

❖ Taking the Initiative

Never believe that you are above the need to be mentored by leaders or those who have journeyed the path before you. You need professors, mentors and 'go-before-us-ers.' In 2 Kings chapter 2 mentorship and its benefits are on classical display. Elisha took the initiative and made a great request of his mentor Elijah to which he responded, 'it is available but in order to receive same, you must see me when I am being taken up.' Elisha got the promise, but he had to be cognizant of some key factors:

I.   In pursuing the blessing, the path will be riddled with discouragement.

II.   It is imperative that you push beyond the negatives.

III.   False prophets may mean well but do stop to listen.

IV.   Sometimes good people can be bad company.

V.   Distraction will cause you to lose sight of the master's vision.

Prayer

Lord, grant me the needed wisdom to decide who must be taken on the journey. Amen

Be encouraged...

When you decide to journey with the Master you will get what the Master got.

DAY 5

LOCKED IN WITH WHO?

ACTS 16:25

Life is punctuated with good and evil. The constant battle between the two for supremacy is never ending. Therefore, when the evil days come knocking with whom will you be locked in? Who will weather the storm with you?

❖ The Evil Days

Through Paul and Silas, a damsel was freed from the evil spirits. However, her masters were angry because the spirit that fed the girl with information was no longer present; hence all possible financial gains were lost. Paul and Silas did an excellent miracle, but their deed was scoffed at, and they were soon thrown in prison. Please be cognizant of the fact that your good

15

work might cause offense, but will you remain faithful to God and to each other during the persecution? According to Acts 16:25 at midnight Paul and Silas prayed and sang praises unto God. They were locked in together, but most importantly, they were locked in with God.

It is imperative that you resist the uprooting of your "locked-in-with-God" by the bulldozer of persecution, sickness and lack.

❖ Rest in Turmoil

The church was being persecuted, James was killed, and Peter was not only placed in prison but was next in line for death (Acts 12:5-11). However, as the church persistently prayed Peter's prison became a place of rest. The saints' prayer was so potent that the angel had to awake Peter from sleep. Who sleeps the night before his or her death? The ability to care for and sacrifice on behalf of another must never be minimized. Your prayer and faith in God will grant someone the confidence to rest amid turmoil.

Key things to consider

1) Adversity is a part of your life and call…
2) Prison is not always for the guilty.
3) In times of lockdown who is with you?
4) Paul was with Silas and Peter was with the guards. Are you locked in with bitterness, anger, judgement, or pride?
5) From a spiritual perspective Paul and Silas were locked in with praise and Peter encapsulated in prayer.

Prayer

Jesus, open my understanding that I may discern with who or what I am locked in. Lord, I pray that I will always be locked in with You. Amen

Be encouraged...

The one with whom you are locked in determines whether or not you leave and how.

DAY 6

STIR IT UP

Acts 17

Wherever we find ourselves, every Christian

has a responsibility to model Jesus. However, as
we model Christ our way of being and our
resistance to unrighteousness and rebellion will
become offensive to others. In fact, simply
speaking against immoral conversations and
acts of injustice, may cause us the unpleasant
and unpopular ire of colleagues, family
members, community, and business leaders.
Nevertheless, we are not called to conform
therefore their response of unease or
persecution should not stop us from being
different.

❖ Dare to be Different

Paul journeyed to Thessalonica to spread the gospel of Jesus. As he taught, the listeners became uncomfortable, and the leaders became distraught. While in your presence, are people comfortable in wrongdoing or do they adjust their behavior? Do you challenge injustice and lying in your immediate environment, or do you let them slide?

Thessalonica was a commercial city and as such the religious leaders became averse to Paul's preaching. Therefore, Paul had to defend the gospel against:

1) Religiosity

Paul made it clear that they needed to be advanced; God had not called them to be basic. 'Do not just come to the synagogue, surrender to the Lordship of Jesus Christ '(Acts 17: 3). It is not enough to 'talk the talk', you must also understand, and 'walk the walk'.

2) Idolatry in the city

The synagogue was in their midst, but the people were still without conviction, confusion still blinded their eyes. Although the streets were filled with people no one stopped to correct their ways or introduce them to the only true God (v.17). Could it be that the sin and error around you have persisted because you have remained silent in your routine? Although Idolatry is rebellion against God it is often due to ignorance, therefore, speak up. If you see something, say something (Phil 4:9). DO SOMETHING! Do not be a private Christian. Level up.

3) Just in case altars (status quo).

When you go to the people of the city; that lost and searching world, you will find a 'just in case people' who need to meet Jesus. Those who visit church to "get a little blessing" or `` pop into the Watch Night Service to get the blessing for the new year. Additionally, those who pray by

21

faith but do not practice the Faith, give them Jesus. Tell them. Feed them. Care for them. Give them Jesus. Judgement is nigh, even at the door (v31). 'And I saw the dead small and great and another book, the book of life where your works are recorded were opened' Rev 20:12. Faith precedes works, but faith without works is dead. Like Jesus Paul stayed busy; he had no chill whatsoever. After stirring the Jews in one place he left to minister to others in another synagogue.

Prayer

Dear Lord, I desire to be used by You. Give me faith. Give me fire. Help me to take the initiative and tell someone about You. Amen

Be encouraged...

Positively stir the place where you are.

DAY 7

IT WILL NOT CHANGE UNTIL YOU DO

Genesis 32:22-31

The beginning of a new year is normally riddled with sentiments of needed change. Persons examine their lives, identify their flaws, and verbally commit to pursuing better. Regrettably, most times the uttered changes are not backed by commitment. Albert Einstein said insanity is repeatedly doing something with the expectation of a different result. Change is what unlocks possibilities. Often, it is not the major but rather minor changes that are required for the realization of the awaited wealth.

❖ **The Wrestling Period**

Jacob and his mother plotted to deceive Esau his brother out of his birthright. The plot was extremely distasteful as it included the deception of his father on his dying bed. Jacob got the blessing from his father through connoving but he had to flee his home for fear of his brother's retaliation. Years later, Jacob made a major change; he wanted a blessing but not by means of deception. Genesis 32:26 states, "and he said, let me go, for the day breaketh. And he (Jacob) said, I will not let thee go, except thou bless me." Jacob's action spoke volumes about the changed person he was and as a result the angel was able to add heaven's change to his life.

❖ **Change of Identity**

In verse 28, the angel said, "Thy name shall be called no more Jacob, but Israel". He got a change of identity. Jacob "supplanter," is often interpreted as someone who seizes,

24

circumvents, or usurps. Israel on the other hand means God contends or one who struggles with God. His name change came with newness and responsibility.

Godly changes accommodate His presence which serves as a coping mechanism and the platform for growth and development. It is difficult to have a genuine encounter with the Lord and not be changed.

❖ What is your answer to prayer?

Answers to prayers are normally accompanied with a requirement to act or change. You either remain as Jacob or change to Israel. What will the needed changes produce in your life? Always remember, God will mobilize what you have and who you are.

Prayer

The change I need to secure my blessed future will be done in the name of Jesus. Amen

Be encouraged...

Failure to change will result in failure to receive newness from God.

DAY 8

STAY IN YOUR LANE

Nehemiah 1

His parents, his teammates, his coaches, the officials who gave him an American flag, 91000 fans at the Bird's Nest watched as Wallace Spearmon scampered around the track for his third-place finish that seemed like first. Then suddenly his bronze medal and time of 19.95 were replaced with a disqualification and when the United States protested Spearman it was said that the athlete lost his medal for stepping outside of his lane along the inside of the curve. After the dust was settled Spearman said, in an interview, I really was not focused on where I was running in the lane. His mistake cost him dearly but Shawn Crawford and Walter Dix, who stayed in their lanes, got second and third behind the world-renowned Usain Bolt.

❖ God needs you where you are

Nehemiah had a coveted but dangerous job. As the king's cupbearer he was charged with tasting everything the king would drink. If poison was set for the king, Nehemiah would be the one to consume it. While Nehemiah's Lane was extremely dangerous, it positioned him to entreat the king for help on behalf of Israel. Your dangerous assignment may just be the position that is keeping your family alive. Stay in your lane.

❖ The Donkey

Jesus needed to travel hence He sent his disciples to retrieve a donkey that no man had ever sat on. The mule was preserved for Jesus. Please understand that what you might consider

28

an overlooking can easily be preservation for purpose. Do not miss the wealth in not being called or invited until your divine kairos moment. Being called before time can easily equate to death.

Nehemiah and the donkey stayed in their lanes and functioned effectively when the need arose. You might not understand why God has you where you are but stay in your God given Lane; it will be worth it. Stop weighing the blessings based on the presenting benefits.

Prayer

Lord thank You for the grace and strength to remain in my lane. Amen

Be encourage...

Stop asking for the PALACE; pray Lord lead me to your PURPOSE.

DAY 9

HOLD YOUR PIECE

{piece /pēs/ a portion of an object or of material, produced by cutting, tearing, or breaking the whole}.

2 Kings 20

Isaiah 39

Hezekiah prayed and asked God to extend his life. However, the extended wealth that came with the answered prayer caused Hezekiah to be blinded to the unholy alliance that awaited him.

❖ **Joseph's Dreams**

Through his dreams, God showed Joseph that he would not only rise to prominence but that he would rule over his family. However, when said information was shared, Joseph's brothers

30

expressed such hatred that they tried killing him and when that was not successful, they sold him into slavery. Joseph's experience has much wealth for us. It teaches that we must hold our piece close to our chest while we carefully contemplate our next move.

❖ Check your friend's list

When Jesus was born, wise men came from the East seeking to worship Him. While they enquired of the babe's location, King Herod instructed them to bring word of the child's whereabouts because he too wanted to worship the King; however, Herod's motive was to kill or destroy the baby. Be vigilant. While you carefully listen to the words spoken in your immediate environment, ask the Holy Spirit to help you to discern the speakers' hearts. Not all platitudes are meant for compliments, sometimes they are simply to get information.

❖ Evil Invitees

"And Hezekiah was glad of them, and shewed them the house of his precious things, the silver, the gold, and the spices, and the precious ointment, and all the house of his armour, and all that was found in his treasures: there was nothing in his house, nor in all his dominion, that Hezekiah shewed them not" (Isaiah 39:2).

Unfortunately, Hezekiah exposed all his possessions to evil' eyes and that caused his demise. Having seen all, the pretenders went away plotted, returned, and looted his kingdom of wealth and personnel. It is important to note that not every eye is worthy of seeing your nakedness. Pride goes before destruction and a haughty spirit before a fall. Be careful. Your ill-conceived action could cost you your life. If you do not kill pride, like Hezekiah it may kill you.

Prayer

Lord, I have tried and failed. Therefore, I ask that you kill my pride. Amen

Be encouraged...

The ability to retain and withhold is more precious than the gift of exposure.

DAY 10

MOVE

Ezekiel 37:1-14

In recent years the abuse of the prophetic has caused extensive bashing of said gifting. However, despite the ridicule and rejection in some circles, the prophetic continues to be relevant.

❖ Instructions Received

God gave Ezekiel instructions regarding the resurrection of the dried bones in the valley. In Verse 4 God told him to prophesy the destiny and the process of what he was going to do, in reverse order [v 5, 6,].

It is easy to miss the move of God because we are not listening or paying attention to His voice.

Therefore, we must be keen listeners when handling the prophetic or lack of expectation will leave us frustrated. When God gives a word, the breakthrough may not be immediate but do not reject the word, something is happening. Although the result may not be forthcoming or the answer may not be what we wanted, receive what God has given for He is perfecting something in us.

❖ Right order, I prophesied as I was commanded

Ezekiel's action produced a powerful truth that can be a liberating genesis for our prosperity; he moved or prophesied as he was commanded. Ezekiel did not rely on selfish motives; he was completely obedient to God. When we move, the stench of self must be totally eradicated by the love of pleasing God. Prophesying without obedience to God is a curse. As he moved in obedience, the desired results were manifested.

A noise, a shaking and the bones came together in their correct order. Then there was sinews, flesh, and skin. Sinews can move bones, but they cannot do so without Adenosine triphosphate (ATP; fuel). Sinews (muscle) get ATP from oxygen, breath or ruach in Hebrew. We are expecting people who have been here for a while, those who have put on "flesh" to move but they are unable to do same because they have no breath.

❖ He 'ruached,' prophesied to the wind…

In all that was done to the bones and sinews they were still not alive…Great results were manifested through the prophetic, but the assignment was incomplete. For the assignment to be completed and the bones move, they needed breath. In order for the assignment to be successfully accomplished the prophet had to move at God's voice and call the wind, breath, to enter the bones. The prophetic will only be effective when the assignment is completed. Could it be that we are presenting window dressing and expecting to be safe when there is no insulation around the window? Complete your assignment and do it God's way. Move, therein is the blessing.

Prayer

Help me Lord to move according to your will amen.

Be encouraged...

Whatever you are doing, do it God's way!

DAY 11

THEN...

Jonah 1

Many bars of defeat have been erected

because many have developed a false

perception that yesterday's obedience is enough

for today. However, in order for obedience to be

effective it must be consistent. Jonah the

prophet of God is mostly assessed as a

backsliding preacher, but that is not the

complete truth. In 2 Kings 14:25 we see the

restoration of the coast of Israel from the

entering of Hamath unto the sea of the plain

according to the words of God which He spoke

through the obedient Jonah. His first assignment

was super successful but then came his second

recorded assignment from God.

❖ He responded in arrogance (heart)

The second assignment exposed Jonah's heart; he responded in arrogance. It is critical that we consistently examine the condition of our hearts. The truth is, God is not surprised at the negative manifestations of our hearts, it is not for His learning but ours. Jonah believed he could run away from God, and we may feel the same as well. However, in his bid to demonstrate His love for us, God will facilitate a situation with the goal of exposing our flaws so that they may be quickly corrected. God knows everything. Stop Running.

❖ Compelled Obedience

After Jonah was gobbled up by the huge fish the narrative changed and reads, "Jonah obeyed the word of the LORD and went to Nineveh (Jonah 3:3)." He shifted drastically from disobedience to obedience not because it was his preference but because God was adamant in using him. God takes the assignments He has given to you seriously as they represent the covenant that is not easily broken. God could have allowed Jonah to drown but His love and mercy gave him three days in what seemed like hell; He received mercy through pain. Let us stop misinterpreting our pain.

❖ The Response

All Nineveh heard the realigned prophet and repented. Never underestimate the wealth and potential of your obedience to God. One message from the rubric of obedience and more than six score thousand persons were spared (120,000). Your assignment is too critical for you to be selfish. Who awaits your obedience? Maybe an individual, family, community, or a nation. Disobedience is too grave an error to make.

40

Prayer

Save me from selfishness and disobedience Lord.

Be encouraged...

Your assignment is bigger than who you are.

DAY 12

DO NOT WATCH THE JOURNEY, WATCH GOD

It is said that the journey of a thousand miles

begins with the first step. However, when we

focus on the distance and begin to complain,

even a forty-day journey seems like forever. As

we navigate the journey, especially the desert,

do not focus on the nothingness, keep your eyes

on God who is leading the way. The path may

appear dry, bones are scattered along but that is

not an indicator that God is dried out. Even in the

desert God remains the oasis; watch Him work.

❖ **Forty Years… foolishness or faith?**

Many of us have started forty-day fasts; some in

pursuit of God while others seek goods.

However, depending on the motive, time is

mostly spent praying, keeping that thing at the center, repetitively asking God to deliver. On the other hand, our motivation may be to receive supernatural power to do exploits for God. Nevertheless, it is most important to understand that time spent in prayer and pursuit of power are not simply to fulfill our purpose but for intimacy with God. 'Seek first the kingdom of God and his righteousness and all, these things will be added to you' (Matthew) 6:33. Draw closer to God, He will draw near to you.

❖ Forget those things which are behind, Run!

The familiarity that comes with captivity can make it more desirable than the uncertainty attached to journeying and finding something new. Theoretically, we love change. We like the idea of expanding our knowledge, sometimes meeting new people and the pride of place when we can say, 'hey look what happened in my prayer closet.' However, in the practical, we become satisfied with what happened. It is easy to talk about what God did, the testimony from last week or the miracle from last year. Nevertheless, it is time. It is time to forget the things of yesterday and rise to greater heights. Do not be deterred by the journey, arise early, and collect the fresh manna. Do not become comfortable in your state. Why continue to go out late to collect that which is insipid and is covered with bird's poop and rodents' footprints? Forget about what was, take what is, take it now.

Prayer

Lord, help me to focus on you and where necessary grant me spiritual blinders that I may move ahead in your will. Amen

Be encouraged...

Relying on God helps to lose the weight.

DAY 13

DO NOT TOUCH THE ARK

2 Samuel 6

It is of utmost importance to remain close to the old landmarks of your belief system or the enlightenment and technological advancement forced on humanity can erode the fundamentals of your faith. Unfortunately, things that were universally accepted as wrong and ungodly are now being instituted as new norms therefore, new is not always the best.

❖ Newness?

In our eyes, Uzzah meant well. After all, the ark was about to fall. Nevertheless, the new

45

transportation did not mean God's instructions had changed. A new cart did not mean the Ark could be touched by every and anyone. We seek and encourage newness; however, if that is all we do then our encouragement and seeking are short sighted; newness desired is not always the will of God. As a result, care must be given in ensuring that all pursued newness is in keeping with righteousness, the right standing with God. Do things God's way.

❖ A "New' Cart

The Ark of the Covenant needed to be returned to its designated area, but special care had to be taken. A new cart was utilized and that seemed like a great idea, but the Ark should be transported on the shoulders of the priests and never by a cart. In the Kingdom of Heaven value and pride must be taken when conducting an assignment. The Ark represented the manifested presence of God; however, through Jesus Christ

46

human beings have become the carriers of His holy presence, but do we treasure this opportunity? On many occasions we relinquish our role and place His presence on presents. Unique, new, does not equate holy use. Consult God first, He knows what He wants.

❖ New Man

As mentioned, Uzzah touched the Ark and God struck him with death. Was God harsh? The truth is we should not handle the things of God simply because it comes naturally; a holy, set apart or person anointed for purpose is required to handle the sacred things. Who shall ascend into the hill of the Lord or stand in his holy place? He who has clean hands and a pure heart. Have you been set apart for the purpose you are pursuing? What is the state of your heart? Let us not miss this truth, disobedience to God cannot be justified nor will it be tolerated by Him, God is holy.

47

❖ *Prayer*

Father in the name of Jesus, help me to give better attention to obedience and cease my desire to justify my sins. Amen

❖ *Be encouraged...*

Obedience, not your help, is all that is required.

DAY 14

WHAT ARE YOU EXPECTING?

Mark 5:35 - 6:20

It is mind boggling that one can experience a mighty move of God yet walk away with unbelief or "half belief," partially believing. In our dispensation, we get accustomed to the shaking, speaking in tongues, the "heat, "the running through church and the Holy Ghost dance as the mighty move of God; yet we scoff at the quiet tears falling. Have our expectations of the power of God become dwarfed or is it a direct manifestation of our lack of knowledge? What are you expecting?

❖ Who is the person?

When you come into the place of worship or a fellowship encounter, who are you expecting to be on display- the man or woman of God or the Holy Spirit? Herein lies the problem: we have made a dangerous paradigm shift from the Holy Spirit to human beings. When our favorite preacher, worship leader or prayer warrior is absent we are unable to engage with the day's lead and that is subtle idolatry. We must get to the place where whether the person presenting is our preferred speaker or not, we understand that the Holy Spirit is present to heal and manifest the power of God.

❖ What is His Purpose?

When you embark on particular days of fasting, what are you expecting? You have a scheduled prayer time for 1:30 every morning but at midnight as you hustle home you are found screaming at a driver who you believe is driving too slowly. There are other times where you are all prayed up but still become frustrated by your partner's actions or all the other hellish things that seem to crash in at the same time. What about all the other issues that have crushed you since prayer? When we say we want to experience the glory of God what exactly is the purpose? Do we want such an enriching praise and worship that cuts into the preaching slot because we do not want the normal shouting that usually comes with the delivery or are we saying the purpose is to see people run to the altar and surrender to the Holy Spirit, to God? We have under-utilized that which Jesus promised and fulfilled to us. The Holy Spirit is the teacher, we must rely on Him to navigate us through the rigors of trials and weaknesses. If we continue to depend on self, we will forever fail.

❖ Where is the power?

Where is the power of God in healing, and deliverance, or is that power only for worship? Could it be that we are not seeing the miracles, signs, wonders and the healing because we are lacking fasting, prayer and spiritual disciplines as directed by the Holy Spirit? Mark chapter 6 says Jesus could only do a few miracles because of the people's unbelief. Yet, He sent His disciples to proliferate miracles so men might see and BELIEVE.

In your next prayer time do not only pray for the Holy Spirit to move, pray for Him to heal, to save and to do miracles that will resonate with you for ages. You have a responsibility to demonstrate the truth to the world; you must be a witness for Jesus. Therefore, as you seek the Holy Spirit for power let it not be for strength just for home duties but for the outdoor move. In the same manner God healed you at home, you must believe that He is able to move upon the brokenness, cancers, blindness and even the dead around you. Let the power of the Holy Spirit be made known mightily through you.

Prayer

Lord I am available to be used by you whenever and wherever you determine.

Be encouraged...

It is not about you.

DAY 15

YOU... WALK

John 5: 8-16

Be careful of "fren and company." The powerful Jamaican idiomatic expression has lived on for generations and simply means do not be too trusting of the crowd or those who are covetous. Unfortunately, we are often quick to leave behind any counsel that sounds like rebuke and seek affirmation in the presence of others because that may be more comfortable. If not well interpreted the love hidden in a rebuke can be mistaken as hatred.

❖ **Who to trust...'fakers' or helpers?**

John 5:8-16 introduces us to an impotent man who spent 38 years at the Pool of Bethsaida. How did he get to the pool? We can safely assume that an individual or a team of persons carried him there; but the help was not enough. In fact, it was more of a punishment for the sick man because they took him to the pool and allowed him to see the truth that people were getting their healing, but he was continuously hindered. They took him to the pool, but they refused to wait with him. We continue to look to those who are around us but, on many occasions, we are left disappointed because they cannot get us in. Stop looking for favors from people and look to God. Some of us WILL NEVER get a handout, or a help out. STOP LOOKING out and LOOK UP.

Look up for your 'help up.' It is better to put your confidence in God than to put your trust in man (Ps 118:8)

❖ Leave it Behind

The text addressed him as being impotent not just lame but then Jesus came on the scene and immediately his thirty-eight years of misery changed. Jesus said, 'You are made WHOLE, sin no more lest a worse thing come upon you' (14). The issue was not a sickness of the body, but a sickness of the spirit, manifesting in the body. That thing you are faced with may not simply be a struggle, it may be a sin. We cannot rebuke away sin, we must surrender it to the Lordship of Jesus Christ and his blood in order to receive forgiveness. Notice James 4:7 says RESIST, not rebuke, the devil and he will flee. We have been rebuking sins we were supposed to be resisting and as a result we have become impotent by them. Could it be that there was some kind of sin that made him impotent? Could it be that your faith is being tried because you waivered? You have found your way to the temple, offered your sacrifice like Cain but somehow your deliverance is being confronted by deceit - DO NOT DO TOUCH SIN! Lest a worse thing come upon you.

❖ When Jesus has healed you, walk!

Verse 11 highlights an important truth. After we have had our encounter with God; move. Do the thing that you could not do before as a demonstration of your deliverance. Immobility causes muscles to atrophy resulting in pressure to regain strength and resume full functioning.

Jesus went against the established protocol for healing. It was the norm for the first person who entered the pool after the angel of the Lord troubled the water to be healed. The rush to enter the water would be generated from the sight realm but Jesus invited the lame man to the faith domain. We must be willing to follow

Jesus' lead. Others had to get wet before healing took place, but all the lame man needed was belief and obedience. Take up your bed and walk, this is a faith journey. There was a large number of infirmed, but Jesus chose the impotent man for a notable miracle. Do not miss out, when Jesus says walk, you walk. Remember, without faith it is impossible to please God. Walking is available. Newness is available but we must be sensitive to the move of God.

Prayer

Lord, help me not to miss my Kairos moment

Be encouraged...

The pain might be long but there is a day of divine intervention.

SECTION 2

FRESH BREAD
&
FLOWING WATER

DAY 16

RIDE YOUR BROKEN PIECES TO SHORE

Acts 27:13-44

Do not be in a hurry to discard or ignore the broken pieces of the journey. Broken crayons are still able to colour excellently. The fact that the whole was broken, and you are left with pieces is a profound sign that there is still hope; use what you have, whole or broken. Acts 27:13-14 states, "And when the south wind blew softly, supposing that they had obtained their purpose, loosing thence, they sailed close by Crete. But not long after, there arose against it a tempestuous wind, called Euroclydon.'

❖ Who Do You Believe?

When the previous verses of Acts 27 are read it is seen that Paul prophesied to the crew. In verse 9 he told them, you are going into dangerous winds, do not leave this port. It was not just about weather; it was about purpose. Throughout the chapter reference is made to weather. The wind was contrary (v4); the wind was preventing them from going quickly (v7); sailing was dangerous (v9) and the wind began blowing softly (v. 13). Very often we allow the external system; weather, circumstances and other happenings to dictate whether it is time to move. We use rituals rather than our relationship with God to determine when and where to go. At other times we become mystical or modern and set out on journeys that the Holy Ghost already told us not to venture on. The truth is most times the soft winds are masking the howling ones that are ahead. As the scripture is examined it shows that Paul saw the danger and unlike Jonah, he revealed to the crew the mind of God for sailing.

Paul was in God's favour so why did they push ahead? Verse eleven shows that the centurion rather believed the owner of the ship than Paul.

❖ The challenge...

Sometimes we experience storms because someone in leadership refused to listen to the command and this has the tendency to throw us into a fit. We may begin fighting leadership because they did not go our way... in churches, in marriages, in offices and many different areas of life. How dare them not to listen? Even if they do not listen to me, how dare them not to listen to God speaking through me? Nevertheless, we must not be turned aside nor become discouraged because we are not heard. It is His will that we do His bidding, and He will take care of the hearts of men.

Prayer

Lord, help me to say what you said to me, even when others are not listening.

Be encouraged...

Stand strong. Say what God said.

DAY 17

SAIL IN THE WORD

Acts 27:1a

It is not the weather but PURPOSE that is

driving the story!

Acts 27:1a "And when it was determined that we

should sail into Italy,"

❖ Purpose

With all the stopping and going, winds howling

and tempest raging, WE ARE GOING TO ITALY!

It is imperative that we stop watching the storm

and watch the WORD! What is the word that

God gave to you? Hold on to that truth for dear

life. Stop watching the warning; it is just a smoke

screen to blind us against the great purpose that

awaits. Remember the warning is not the word... it is a caution, and an invitation to exercise faith in the Word.

❖ Condition

It sounds good to say thus saith the Lord, 'I am going to destroy you, but we do not pay much attention to the last part... "if you do not stop." If you do not stop is a condition which indicates the real object lesson - GOD INTENDS TO SAVE! God intends to COMPLETE THE MISSION. God desires to get you to your PURPOSE! Therefore, you cannot afford to be distracted by the warning... the warning is just weather, it is simply wind!

Do not get thrown off because your boss or your business partner is not listening, and the business is about to hit rock bottom. You may have recommended going digital even before you knew a major crisis was coming. Now instead of sailing through, the business is on the verge of crashing but keep trusting. Keep watching, keep sailing... YOU ARE ON YOUR WAY TO PURPOSE!!!! And NOTHING CAN STOP GOD'S WILL!

Prayer

Lord, as You lead me to purpose, teach me to keep my eyes on your hands. Amen

Be encouraged...

Delay does not mean denied.

DAY 18

BROKEN? STAY WHEELING.

Acts 27:13-44

God's Mind

God sent Jeremiah down to the potter's house to help us understand a deep truth about the mind of God. Many people think that their prayers are powerful enough to change the mind of God, however, unless those prayers are in alignment with His purpose and plan, NO CHANGE WILL HAPPEN! Change is only manifested in our circumstances; God never changes His mind. The change that we experience God allowed it; He always knew it would happen.

67

James 4:2-3 says, 'you have not because you ask not, and when you ask you ask to consume it on what you want...' While the text is true, unanswered prayers can easily lead to frustration and we blame it on, God is not ready. However, it is not that God is not ready... God is saying, IT IS NOT GOING TO HAPPEN! It is not His PURPOSE OR PLAN. Get used to accepting God's NO. No does not mean, not yet No means No.

❖ **The Precursor**

Jeremiah 18: verse 3b ... I saw him working at the wheel... and the pot that he was making became marred in his hands...v4.

The first part is easy for us, we can see the pot being shaped. Nevertheless, long before the formation of the pot there was the part that Jeremiah did not see; the preparation, getting and wetting the clay, starting the machine. In the olden days labour was only manual. Arduous work went ahead of the final product. PROCESS PRECEDES PURPOSE. As we examine the text through Jeremiah's lenses, we see that God was still working on the clay; it was still on the wheel. If God is still working on the wheel and still fashioning the clay, we can easily apply that outlook to the story in Acts 27 and conclude that weather and wind are simply the precursors to the purpose. YOU ARE GOING TO ITALY.

Jeremiah's participation in the progressive revelation caused him to make assumptions about the potter's intention and we do that at times. It looks like it is becoming a pot, so we latch on to that seeming fact without the understanding that it is just one of the stages leading to the purpose. When you see the pot as the end product, purpose, and things change you say things like, 'the pot he was making became marred in the hand of the potter.' Who said the potter intended to build a pot or what it looked like when you saw it?

You walk into the kitchen and your spouse is kneading dough. However, if kids are involved the shape of that dough could morph into one hundred different characters. In fact the very product would be characters that are means to achieve the purpose. The final product is the meal... a johnny cake meal, boiled dumplings, or crust for the pizza, the possibilities are endless. It could even be an art project. Never try to assume with God only He knows the final product.

Prayer

Lord, help me to hear your heart and not be discouraged by your working hand. If change should come oh help me be surrendered my dear Lord to Thee.

Be encouraged...

"O let my trembling soul be still,

And wait thy wise, thy holy will!

I cannot, Lord, thy purpose see,

Yet all is well since ruled by thee."

~ Spurgeon

DAY 19

NEWNESS IS IN GOD'S MIND

Acts 27:13-44
Jeremiah 18:3b

Can you by searching find out God? His ways

and thoughts are higher than ours. Yet instead of

trusting Him to work out the details we expend a

great deal of energy trying to understand and

know what He is doing.

❖ **Newness**

Jeremiah 18:3b declares, he made it again

another vessel, AS IT SEEMED FIT FOR HIM

TO MAKE IT. This time Jeremiah did not

describe the 'another vessel'... he understood

the POINT, that was the secret, the revelation

God was giving about Himself... HE IS IN THE

BUSINESS OF FORMING PEOPLE FOR HIS PURPOSE. In some instances, you may appear as though you are a particular design but soon after you become something else. Do not remain stuck and do not jump off the wheel; it is just a stage in the process. ...as it seemed fit for him to make it... focus on the PURPOSE and not the WIND, the process.

Let us reflect on Acts 27

Maybe it is not the boss or business partner that did not listen. It could be your spouse, he or she did not take your dream seriously and now trust has been severed because this is not the first time. When you got married the union looked like The Rock but now it looks like Mr Bean; lack of trust has worn out the muscles. It may be too that at the beginning of the union you resembled J Lo but now you look like Jane from the jungle; you changed. On the other hand, things maybe perfect at home but church is driving you up the wall. Over and over, you have been warning the

73

choir director about "that person." You told the pastor something is not right, you sensed it in your spirit; you received the word, and you gave the warning and still they set out "to sail" and now they are in Euroclydon (v14). How about your personal life? What has God been saying but you have not listened? It could be that you have put forth a fleece which came back, and you are saying, "LORD IF YOU SHOW ME THIS SIGN then I will…," but He is showing the sign, soft wind, v13. Yes, you have set sail and are now in the wind but stay on board; sailing is not always easy. The winds and waves are whacky but won't watch the wind. It's only a warning, the wind is only part of the process.

DAY 20

YOU WILL GET TO THE SHORE

Acts 27:13-44

Never confuse miracles for might. Reminder,

Pharoah's magicians also threw down their rods
and they too became snakes like that of Moses'.
The blessing is not in things or smooth sailing
but the miracle in which you arrive at the shore.
The blessing is God being with you in the storm,
in the secret place of the Most High. It is
standing before Caesar and declaring the mind
of God; that is the purpose. Do not become
confused by all the happenings around you.
Things may be going well but is God with you, is
He your compass and shield? Never believe that
the storm is a sign that you are operating under
a curse.

75

❖ Foolishness

The centurion preferred to listen to the owner, the very one who led the sailors to cast the luggage overboard and threatened to kill the prisoners, then to Paul. Yet Paul told them all the furor was foolishness; except they abode in the ship they would not be saved. Casting of, making the ship lighter, FOOLISHNESS. A broken ship is not an automatic death sentence. Many people died when the Titanic sank, but the unexpected happened as well, MANY PEOPLE LIVED! The difference between faith and foolishness is the WORD. Paul said, 'this night the angel of the Lord appeared to me.' Do not get into a frenzy from what others are predicting or even what flesh is showing you; if you do, you will jump overboard. Stay on the ship. Even though it is going to be ripped apart, God's presence will ensure the blessing!

Do not watch the wind, watch His PURPOSE. God does not move according to rhyme and reason, so STOP IT. Stop fashioning God in your image and likeness; It is YOU who ought to be formed according to HIS. We sometimes stop doing what we are called to do because we were criticized and told that what we are saying is foolishness but quickly respond to the fear of foolishness with the foolishness of faith, "except you abide in the ship you cannot be saved."

You do not need to be able to swim to survive this season

Stop watching the wind and do not put trust in the ship. Rest in the word, 'the angel of the Lord appeared to me this night.' I understand. The word seems crazy because the ship is torn apart, you are treading water, and everyone is saying you are going to drown. However, it is not your ability to swim, romance, rhyme or reason that will keep you through the seas... IT IS THE WORD... THE PURPOSE! So even if you are on broken pieces, ride them to shore. The blessing is in the fact that even in the storm the journey to Italy must be materialized.

Whatever aspect of your life is on the rock, broken marriage, business, church or even your personal life and the Word (prophecy, purpose) says you will be happy. Although it sounds foolish and your friends and family are saying such pain could not be God's will, stay in the ship. God moves by purpose. Never forget, the period from Genesis chapter 1 to Matthew was simply a PROCESS! What process? Preparing the way for Jesus. Pot for purpose, another vessel as it seems fit, the purpose was JESUS! Jesus was sent to save! It might take one hundred days, one hundred or even one thousand years, His purpose remains the same. Your purpose might take you up on Mount Moriah, it might enslave you in Egypt or allow you to build a temple and tear the walls down or take you to a ship that gets broken in a storm. Whatever the situation, stay on board and if the ship gets broken, ride your broken pieces to shore.

Prayer

HELP!

Be encouraged...

Keep walking by the word and not by watching the wind...

DAY 21

HAVE IT HIS WAY

Num 22:5; 24:2

2 Pet2:15

Rev 2:14

The path to sin begins with compromise which when, fueled by pride, leads to idolatry that is often followed by porneia, the New Testament for sexual immorality. Such compromise has allowed Witchcraft to become rampant in the church of God. Sadly, it is not just among the suspecting but even among the very "prophets", the good ones, the ones who hear from the Lord. There are many who have a spiritual gift and have made it into wizardry. In Numbers 22 Balaam who had a connection with God and was considered a prophet was consumed with witchcraft. My friend, such false righteousness leads to deeper unrighteousness. Balaam made his prophetic anointing into witchcraft and tried bringing God onboard by teaching Balak to cast a stumbling block, support idolatry and sexual perversion.

Issues

❖ **Demands**

Unrighteous profiteers have a particularly common trait in that they demand or rather "convict" offering from people by inviting them to sow seeds to activate their faith and that the seed will deliver a miracle. Nevertheless, people will do all that they demand and are still poor, still not promoted, still going to the doctors, indebted, and frustrated because all their money was squandered. While the word of God says faith cometh by hearing and hearing the word of the Lord. Healing comes when we believe, and deliverance comes when we speak the name of Jesus. In the New Testament the blind man asked alms of the disciples but instead of heeding they led him to an encounter with divine healing, no charge nor any money exchanged.

Does giving an offering release a blessing? Yes, it does, it is a universal principle; it is more blessed to give than to receive, Acts 20:35. When you give what you are holding becomes less and sometimes your hand is left empty. Therefore, by your giving you activate your capacity to receive. However, when giving is done simply to receive a blessing from God you are make the giving into witchcraft as though the return that comes to you is because of the quality of your giving.

❖ Giving in obedience brings blessing.

Balaam thought he could sacrifice that which he had and received God's instruction. Let us be careful. Giving to activate God may engage demons instead. We cannot, even by giving, control God. Our sacrifice will never change God's mind or force His hand to act on our behalf. Jesus already died once FOR ALL. It is only through Jesus that we can state a claim before God, only Jesus and the things of Him can move the Father. Our fasting and praying for seven or twenty-one days do not in and of themselves impress God... God is 'faithed' to act by the life that says HAVE YOUR WAY. God wants us to come to such a place where we are no longer saying here is what I want but give me what you have for me. He wants us to say THY WILL BE DONE (Luke 22:42).

Prayer

Father in the name of Jesus, let your will be done. Help me to get this right and no longer be deceived amen.

Be encouraged...

Sin is enticing but we should not be entertained or succumb to it. God has provided what you need to escape the claws of sin and death. You are victorious through Jesus. Let no man deceive your gifts from your care.

DAY 22

SEER OR SEER?

Numbers 22:1-12

We easily take our reputation for granted. We misuse the maxim, character over reputation. However, one's reputation can be the determining factor between a closed or opened door. In the story with Balaam his reputation preceded him, but it was poor. Every time the story of God's favor to Israel is told, Baalam and his Father's name are mentioned in a negative way. What are you known for? What is mentioned about you when your name is called?

❖ **Contrast**

In one of the verses, Balaam was known as a prophet but in another as a diviner. Such contrast forced me to dig a little about Balaam and I found that many of us are controlled by a similar spirit. The prophet was WORLDLY! He was out of focus. He had a form of godliness but denied the power that was needed. Although we are gifted and anointed there is a struggle with THE FLESH, and it is not necessarily sexual. Struggle with the flesh has to do with anything that emerges from within us that is in opposition to the work of the Spirit, God, within you.

❖ Flesh exposed

The works of the flesh might be pride, greed, mammon, money, gluttony, malice, envy, unforgiveness, selfishness, hypocrisy, being FAKE, being judgmental, pride, false righteousness, WITCHCRAFT, including rebellion - both personal and leading others along the same path, disobedience, laziness and so on... when we hear about struggles with the flesh let us pay keen attention.

Contextually speaking, Diviner or seer is a common reference for one who has the gift of "seeing". However, to refer to him, a prophet of the Lord as a diviner was to make his gift common or might have referred to his familiarity or his reputation of taking gain or profit from his gifting. Therefore, the reference as diviner seems to ask the question of Balaam, are you a prophet or for profit? Although we are anointed when we reduce the gifts of God to personal profit, money or otherwise, we expose ourselves to satanic influence, or satanic oppression. Additionally, the common outcome is that divination, the practice of being a diviner, could be the enemy of our souls. It is important for us to recognize that our fallenness often has an enabler, someone who the enemy has in waiting, or someone who might be vulnerable, waiting for that moment of weakness to cause the stars to align and pull us in. Remember I said weaknesses of the flesh is not only sexual. The devil knows that he cannot trap you that way, but your weakness is not hidden.

We talk about secret struggles but there are no struggles that are truly secret. Jesus says whatever is inside us will come out. The corrupt reputation came about because of corrupt behavior. There are demonic spotters who quickly identify the "secret" and have specially "trained helpers" ready to align with you to practice without judgement. As true followers of Jesus, we must refrain from following blindly. Not every time the prophet, diviner, says "lift your hand and say…", "point to your neighbor and say…", "touch yourself and say…", should we latch on to every word. When we do so, we enable much of the foolishness that takes place in church. We call them movements of the Spirit but on many occasions, they are exorbitant displays of the flesh and familiar stroking of our emotions by underprepared, losing their anointing used to be seers.

.   Idolatry

We may think we are not practicing idolatry because we are not falling and worshipping the prophet. However, if we ignore the spirit of discernment but gullibly accept everything done or said by the prophet, diviner, Man or Woman of God, it can easily be idolatry. Please note the text never indicated that Balaam was being led by an evil spirit; what we see at work is bad behavior from an unruly character. Therefore, what he needed was not deliverance but a change in behavior. What is your state? What spiritual bad habits do you need to break? Some things do not need deliverance, fasting and prayer will only help when you begin to use the power of surrender to deny yourself and let the word work.

PRAYER

I declare in the name of Jesus that I will forever use my gifts for the glory and enhancement of God and His Kingdom. Amen

Be encouraged...

Not every prophet is seeing through the Spirit of God; some are seeing through intelligence, experience, training, charms, crystal balls and demons.

DAY 23

MY GIFT, HIS GLORY

2 Peter 2:14

Based on Balaam's reputation one would think that he would fade into irrelevance. However, his name is mentioned on many occasions both in the Old and New Testament.

❖ Visibility

His behaviour is recorded in Numbers chapters 22, 24, Deuteronomy 23, Joshua 13, Micah 6 and 2 Peter 2. As we read the texts, we realize that he became an example of WHAT NOT TO DO as a prophet. Just because somebody shows up in critical places does not mean they have good intentions. Buyer beware. Let us look at the New Testament reference in 2 Peter 2:14ff.

Their eyes are full of adultery; their desire for sin is never satisfied; they seduce the unstable. They are accursed children with hearts trained in greed. 15They have left the straightway and wandered off to follow the way of Balaam son of Beor, who loved the wages of wickedness. 16But he was rebuked for his transgression by a donkey, otherwise without speech, that spoke with a man's voice and restrained the prophet's madness

❖ (Balaaming) in our time...

Let us take another look at Balaam as we remove the veil and uncover the truth. The story goes on to tell us that Balaam persisted with his quest to get the money and walked as close a line as he could to "do the will of God". Can you see the evil? Many of us are trying to bargain with the flesh and walk in the Spirit. Can you imagine how much some diviners would charge for the weight of the anointing that is on your life?

Another aspect of Balaaming is the acceptance of the limitations placed on us when given an invitation to preach or teach the word or lead a small group. Many of us have taken the liberty where none was given; speaking well beyond the time that was allocated and WELLLLLLL beyond what God said. We are very much in the spirit but fighting flesh. Limitations such as a nudge to raise the offering for the night or we will not be paid, or the hint that the crusade is struggling or the conference did not garner as much as planned, a hint you may not be "paid." So instead of moving in the anointing of the assignment, experience snaps in to raise an offering to ensure the people give because people will support the visiting speaker when they are "blessed." It is high time for us to stop falling prey to the use of gimmicks, groans, music, or the right song. We mimic television prophets because they have set the tone for what the anointing looks like. When no one falls when we lay hands, we feel the room is not ready or we were not "successful" and we measure the next prophet by that rubric. On the other hand, we become satisfied with the fall out, trembling lips and voice, whooping measure then the prophet leaves and we remain dry, wondering and waiting for the next prophet to come without realizing it is the truth of God's Word that makes us free, not the feeling and falling. We must get to the place where we weigh the prophet by the manifestation of the Spirit, the word of truth, real signs, and wonders. A clear distinction is being highlighted- real signs. We become afraid to believe for healing in the church because Satan has come among us and made us skeptical and judgmental instead of discerning.

❖ It's not just them it is also us

We are looking at all the gullible people but what about our silence? What about our words of rebuke we "race up people," Jamaican vernacular, or pump-up people in times of worship. It is often said, "if you praise him the blessing will come down;" but that is a direct misrepresentation of the living God. The Creator of the universe is in the room, and He is the reason we came; it is His blessing that brought us together. The blessing is already there! This is one of the reasons some people will not worship because they are living on the mercy drops while thinking that if they give a little more, they will get a little more. We are balaaming when we try to play boatie (two sides).

Prayer

I declare in the name of Jesus that I will forever use my gifts for the glory and enhancement of God and the Kingdom of God. Lord, I want more of you. Pull me closer, take me further, take me deeper. Amen

Be Encourage...

It is easier to change your mind than to force God's hand. Let go, let God.

DAY 24

LISTEN TO YOUR ASS

Numbers 22: 1-12; 21

We are daily bombarded with people, animals

and things craving our attention; some seek our

words while others our ears. However, as you

ponder on the statement would you listen to

either of the four below?

"Jack"   Donkey

Jackass   Village idiot

You may say are you crazy but do not answer

just yet, think about it... would you? We, the

limited, frail human, are prone to sin but through

the Spirit of the Living GOD inside of us, we are

also given LIMITLESS POWER that has increased our ability to hear.

❖ Listen to your ass

In our response to the first question many would not listen to the village idiot, the donkey, a jackass or even "Jack" because we "talk to God on the regular." The projected attitude is, why would God talk to you, instead of me when He and I are not in malice. Why should I listen to Jack? This jackass is trying to keep me from my blessings. This jackass does not have the intelligence I have so how dare her, him or it try to slow me down? Please understand that your jackass may not have gotten to the speaking stage yet, but the fact that you are balaaming, going into battle with armor you have not proven, getting up unconsecrated and presenting a word you heard from last week without asking God for the daily bread. Trials and temptations, family sickness and spousal disagreement are just some of the many demands on you that have refused to be reduced. You have begun asking the famous question, 'what is happening' followed by a series of rebukes to Satan. However, is it possible that the turbulence, the upheaval, the stormy weather, the squeezing against the wall is a prompting to listen to your ass? Balaam noticed that his ass was operating in a manner that was not conducive with his desires, yet he failed to receive the message that was being conveyed by the animal.

❖ The voice in your situation

Listen to your ass. Maybe, just maybe, God is using your situation to speak to you. Listen, because the false righteousness, spiritual snobbery about who can or cannot bring a word to you, will only lead to deeper unrighteousness. Avoid the error of Balaam who persisted against the entreating of God and almost lost his life. The fact that you have not yet been punished does not mean you will always have the same fortune. Do not trust sly, slick, or slippery to keep you out of trouble. Listen to your jackass, he may save your life.

There is a move of God in this season, but if we do not deal with the distractions, bargaining, gimmicks, pageantry, and power-struggle, we will be left behind or even killed. At first glance, it seemed as though God was directing Balaam, giving him answers to take back to Balak. However, when we listen to the commentary throughout the Bible about Balaam and the response of the angel, we realize that Balaam was not really on God's mission. Instead, he found himself pushing against the will of God, and God allowed him to come face to face with the result of lack of wisdom and an unsurrendered life. From the get-go Balaam knew he could not curse God's people but for the gain he persisted. What are you pushing against God to get? Who are you pushing against God to have? What are you pursuing under the dark cover of the night, away from the watchful eyes who would give you wise feedback, though negating what you want? What? Who? Where? When?

❖ Balaam's talking ass

27 When the donkey saw the angel of the LORD, it lay down under Balaam, and he was angry and beat it with his staff. 28 Then the LORD opened the donkey's mouth, and it said to Balaam, "What have I done to you to make you beat me these three times?"

29 Balaam answered the donkey, "You have made a fool of me! If only I had a sword in my hand, I would kill you right now." 30 The donkey said to Balaam, "Am I not your own donkey, which you have always ridden, to this day? Have I been in the habit of doing this to you?" "No," he said. 31 Then the LORD opened Balaam's eyes, and he saw the angel of the LORD standing in

the road with his sword drawn. So, he bowed low and fell facedown.32 The angel of the LORD asked him, "Why have you beaten your donkey these three times? I have come here to oppose you because your path is a reckless one before me. [a] 33 The donkey saw me and turned away from me these three times. If it had not turned away, I would certainly have killed you by now, but I would have spared it."

God revealed to Balaam that if it was not for his ass, he would have been dead. In the end Balaam escaped the sword of the angel of the Lord but he did not escape the donkey's voice. Unless you change your direction, whatever you run from will catch up with you and that is all your ass is trying to tell you. 'There is a way that seems right unto a man, but the end thereof are the ways of death' Prov 14:12. The rejection to change and pursue the way of God's will always leads to death.

Prayer

Show me your will oh God. Grant me wisdom to yield to your directions that I may live and not die. Additionally, Lord, help me not to despise the vessel You have chosen to use but please help me to listen as You speak and humbly surrender. Amen

Be encouraged...

You could lose your life by moving on. Change direction. Trust your ass.

DAY 25

ENTICEMENT

Gen 39:4-7

At first glance and because of the setting and familiarity of the story we see sex, or a scene of seduction playing out before our very eyes. It is fascinating but it is a facade. Yet we sit with it, we preach on it, we pound it out because sexual immorality and sexual impropriety are quite the hangman's noose of Christians and many men and women of God get caught in ii as well. However, as we excavate the text, we find a revelatory reminder that goes beyond the sexual drama.

Potiphar's wife, the seductress, is easily identified but what is hidden is the seducing spirit that propels her. It is not immediately plain in the text before us, but the Apostle Paul helps us to understand the applicability of the concept to this context. In Ephesians chapter 6:10-18 he reminds us that we wrestle not against flesh and blood (seductress) but against spirits.

❖ Truth

From a deeper perspective we see three devices or strategies that the serpent uses against us in the struggle with the seed of the woman. His primary approach or role is that of an accuser. In this text we can see him manifesting his three-step strategy to defeating God's elect. It is necessary for us to remove the veil of the seductress because I do not want us to be hypnotized by her charm. Lest we miss the head of the serpent at work under her skin let us go deeper.

❖ Enticement (verse 7)

This is an age-old strategy and simply means something used to attract or to lure someone. Please note that for something to be qualified as an enticement it must be attractive and appear to be relevant to the unsuspecting potential.

Genesis 3 - Eve and Adam

The serpent said to the woman, "You will not certainly die," For God knows that when you eat from it your eyes will be opened, and you will be like God, knowing good and evil."

Look at the devil's enticement. First, he removed the boundaries by discrediting God, You will not certainly die. In other words, God lied. The serpent was trying to convince Eve and Adam that God wanted to keep them below the level of who they really were. In essence, there is more to you than what God has told you. Second, the serpent presented the enticement in a carefully laid out package. "Your eyes shall be opened' but were they blind? and you shall be like God knowing good and evil." Knowing the magnificent display of God, who would not want to be like Him?

Mathew 4... Jesus

After forty days fasting in the wilderness Jesus was hungry. Satan presented a sensible attractive enticement, 'turn these stones into bread'. He knew Jesus was hungry and that he had the power and authority to do the conversion. However, Jesus rejected the pull.

Genesis 39 - Joseph

❖ Run

For the unsuspecting, do not think that the only seduction in the devil's bag are the fruit and bread also known as sex. The devil knows that he cannot use those to entice you but please understand that it does not mean he will not try. For some of us the lure is in the seduction itself while for others like Joseph the lure was the invitation to treat or the quest to satisfy HER THIRST, not his. His trouble was going to be the power and pride of place that came from being positioned with pageantry. The seducing spirits were successful against Samson, but Joseph had A SINGLE RESPONSIBILITY do not fall for the enticement. Any ordinary slave would have been enticed by such a powerful offer. However, Joseph was not an ordinary guy; he had dreams and visions that were bigger than himself and Potiphar's wife. As you read, whether male or female, do not allow the enticement from the powerful to play you. It looks good but you are being offered something that is neither theirs to give nor yours to take. RUN.

Some of us are in the face of danger because we have courageously decided to make a valiant stand to resist whatever the entreaty but let us not believe that we are intellectual enough to argue our way out of the coy of a centuries-old demon who has been around the track. The cloak of enticement does not always look the same way for everyone:

- It could be a speaking engagement
- A job offer
- A business deal

Examine the package carefully. Are you being asked to compromise your values, to break some rule of law? If yes, It is not an opportunity, it is a devil – RUN.

Prayer

Dear Lord, sometimes my feet get heavy, and my eyes become transfixed on the enticements around me but help me to keep my focus on you and lose my feet to run. Amen

Be encouraged...

The beginning point of a fallen life is often in the decision to stand or to run. If you have to decide when your integrity is at stake, choose to run.

DAY 26

ENTRAPMENT

Gen 39:11-12

A soldier with one bullet is desperate and might be an easy defeat if not given swift reinforcement; the spirit of seduction knows this and has equipped itself not only with enticement but also entrapment. What is entrapment? It is a practice in which a law enforcement agent or agent of the state induces a person to commit a "crime" that he or she would have otherwise been unlikely or unwilling to do.

The serpent's second device we see is:

❖ **ENTRAPMENT (verses 11- 12)**

When the woman saw that her seduction was not working, she decided to up the ante and bring out the big guns; 'Lie with me OR Else'. Where the enemy cannot entice he will try to entrap you. The seductress in the text realized that the charms of seduction were failing so she seized an opportunity when the keepers of the house were out to make a violent move against Joseph. Sounds familiar? Out of nowhere all the smooth talk, all the loving action, all the gifts and charm make way for threats and ultimatums. Sometimes it is coy and at other times it is overt; the truth is it can be unnerving, unsettling, and frightful.

However, if God be for us, WHO can be against and be victorious. Be mindful though, you cannot stand there and talk or 'blood of Jesus' your way out of the likely trap, RUN. We have an intercessor also called an ADVOCATE (paraclete), also known as an attorney, LEGAL representation who will speak on our behalf. I am not schooled in law, but I understand enough to know that judges are not happy with people who represent themselves especially when they

112

believe that they know the law but are in fact lacking with court procedures and the breadth of law in the matter they are bringing before the court. When you have a legal impediment, it is to your advantage to have an advocate speak on your behalf, then you will be advised when to or if you should speak. I know, under normal circumstances you are not supposed to leave the scene of a crime, but if your ADVOCATE advises you to do so – RUN WITHOUT QUESTIONING.

 Today the PARACELTE (advocate) has information you do not have. He is aware that the accuser of the brethren, Satan, has brought an accusation against you in the courts of heaven and has sent a reminder through this officer of the court to let you know representation is already being brought on your behalf- and YOU HAVE THE RIGHT TO REMAIN SILENT, but do not just stand there, RUN.

Prayer

O LORD, how my foes have increased! How many have risen up against me! Many say of me, "God will not deliver him." But You, O LORD, are a shield around me, my glory, and the One who lifts my head. Therefore, the trap of the fowler laid again me will collapse before it ensnares me. Hallelujah. Amen.

Be encouraged...

He makes my feet like hinds' feet able to stand firmly and tread safely on paths of testing and trouble; He sets me securely upon my high places.

DAY 27

ENSNAREMENT

Genesis 39: 13-16

A well thought out plan will not end at

entrapment but will follow through with

ensnarement. Ensnarement is that final blow in

ensuring that the victim is found guilty and

sentenced. Please be conscious that Satan or

the spirit propelling the seductress does not

believe he will fail. You can be sure he knows

the entrapment will not work, so he will start the

powerplay. The Jamaican proverb states, ' If you

caan ketch Quako yuh ketch him shut, when an

enemy cannot get to you they will reach for

those close to you. When the spirit tried to

entrap Joseph but he would not lie with her, the

game plan against him shifted, it was now to

get evidence against him that would be used for ensnarement.

❖ Ensnarement

The reinforced plot to ensure that Joseph is hurt. The spirit behind the seductress was willing to accept failure at getting him to be intimate with her but was not willing to see him go without pain. The plot was never about him having sex with her, it was always to destroy his relationship with God and thus his dreams. The ensnarement was the final step in the plan to mess up Joseph. After all the journey he had made, thinking his dreams were closer to reality only to be cast into a dark dungeon with criminals on both sides. Sounds familiar? Think about Christ on the cross. Today if you are faced with such a situation do not feel any shame whatsoever, put your foot in your hand and RUN. Flee speedily from the house of temptation to the house of blessings. It may first be a padlocked door of limitation, but God only has you there to make the right connections as he executes his foolproof plan.

❖ Please do not ignore this

Joseph ran! To the undiscerning eye, not seeing through the spirit, he might look guilty. If running makes you look guilty, run anyway.
Nevertheless, as with Joseph, running does not mean favour, someone coming to your defense or escaping prison but still decide to run. If you still do not believe that the active play against you is more than what meets the eye, more than the sexual seductions that the temptress was presenting - hear me my friend, behind every temptress is a tempter! There are bigger cards at play than you think. DO NOT FALL FOR IT!!

❖ **Resist**

If the charming alliance; offer of marriage seems too good to be true, IT IS IN FACT not true. Do not ignore the warning signs, it is time to check in with GOD and THE HOLY GHOST. The Holy Ghost has some information on that offer you have not yet received. Psalm 91:3 helps us to understand the purpose of the ensnarement, 'Surely, he shall deliver me from the snare, ensnarement, of the fowler.' Who is a fowler? One who catches fowls. What is a fowl? A bird. You, precious one, POWERFUL one, you are not a fowl of the ground, you are a bird. You belong in the sky, to soar in the high heavens - that is what God says about you. 'You who wait on the Lord will mount up on wings like EAGLES! That is the reason the fowler wants to catch you; he wants to ground you and clip your wings that you will never fly. It is said that when an eagle is battling a serpent, it does not struggle with its prey. Instead it picks it up and soars into the sky because the eagle knows when the serpent goes past a certain altitude and fast enough, it will pass out.

Well, my EAGLE brother, my EAGLE sister, the Bible says, he has raised us up and caused us to sit together in heavenly places in Christ Jesus. The serpent does not want us in that height, he wants that height so he can maintain spiritual wickedness in high places. Today let us stand firm and say not so - my soul shall escape like a bird out of the snare of the fowler. Birds do not run, they fly, so we could easily change the focus thought from RUN and still capture the same meaning. However, since the text we are speaking directly deals with feet do not cower under the snare of the fowler, RUN

Prayer

O Lord my feet sometimes wander and from weariness begin to slip. Please help me not to stumble and get stuck beneath the ensnarement of the wicked one. Lord, deliver me. Amen

Be encouraged...

They that wait upon the Lord shall renew their strength. Do not wait there, RUN.

DAY 28

EMBRACE THE WORD

2 Timothy 4:2-8

Remember the number 1 survival skill,

"condition your mind before you condition your body." I think we have known for a while that the spiritual battleground is the mind and this propels us to go to prophetic conferences, sign up for daily Bible readings and "positive" quotes. We even separate ourselves from the "haters" and say goodbye to negative people, thinking that by doing these things, we have won. However, after the grueling fight we return from the stadium with torn hamstrings, back spasms and the hip out of joint BECAUSE listening to scripture does not serve its purpose if we do not allow the word to change us from the inside out.

Starting with the mind

The power of the word is latent, possessing potential to transform, but it requires activation. The Sower in Matthew 13 released his seeds and the ones that produced were the ones that were activated by the soil on which they fell. A good word requires a good (clean) heart to become activated and produce purpose. Are you taking the time to cultivate the soil of your heart to make it ready for the word? Are you removing distractions (DND on the phone, entering a private room (secluded place) or closet)? Are you ridding yourself of disagreements and indiscipline? Are you taking time to meditate, write and recite the word?

Israel was told to use the word in their architectural processes, place it over your doorposts), then God took it a little farther and said, 'WRITE IT UPON THE TABLETS OF YOUR HEART, It is His word that cleanses the heart. It is the word that is a lamp to our feet, and a light to our pathway. When our feet are well lit, shod with the preparation of the gospel of peace, we can avoid obstacles whether small or large as such a pathway helps us to see lurking dangers and the way to turn. Light turns darkness into day.

Paul encouraged the Philippian believers, chapter 2:5-11, "Let this mind be in you which was also in Christ Jesus..." The mind of Christ was filled with wisdom, the knowledge of God and compassion for humanity as a demonstration of the Lord of God poured out. We should therefore measure our response by matching our mind, manifested by our thoughts and behavior, with that of Christ. Yet Paul did not stop with matching the mind of Christ but entreated the young Timothy (2 Tim 4:2-8) to model the mind of Christ. To model the mind of Christ, Paul entreated Timothy to exercise the word. Preach it. Reprove from it. Rebuke from it. Exhort from it (with mindfulness and patience). Doctrine from it because the way the word is received today may not be the way it is received tomorrow. However, the people who know the word will respond rightly with the word of truth rather than believing a lie.

❖ Embracing the word, condition your mind

The Miriam-Webster online dictionary, Britannica also agrees, that conditioning is the process in which the body, or particular muscle groups, is put through a specific set of exercises, diet and rest so that those muscles acclimatize to increased pressure with a view to optimize performance. Paul also reminded the believers in Rome not to be confirmed to this world and its system of belief or philosophies but to be transformed by the renewing of their mind. Train your mind to think God's thoughts. It is not enough to be righteous. It is not enough to even be Godly. God wants us to return to a place of surrender so that we may become obedient.

124

Obedience is that place where we will do it God's way without rebellion.

❖ Condition your body

Fasting and prayer is the process of denying the flesh certain pleasantries so that the spirit man may develop resistance and endurance. When we are able to overcome the pangs of hunger and stay focused long enough to pray, we will find that we begin to move into a different realm of revelation. Denying the body food for a period we prescribe is an act of empowering the mind and spirit to master or give instruction to the body, rather than the body restricting the mind and spirit because of its limitations. How often do we fall asleep while reading the scripture or praying? However, when the body is under subjection, we discipline the mind to get enough sleep and to keep a regular sleep pattern so that we are well rested.

When the body is fully rested it has no excuse to stay awake and a renewed mind will always be ready for spiritual engagement. When we are conditioned in said manner not only are we denying ourselves food but also satisfaction that would otherwise strengthen us to forsake or resist the lure of sin and the sinner. The truth is many persons who succumb to the lure of seduction or sexual impurity did not fall because of sexual desires enticing them to express (sin); they were always able to keep the sexual proclivities at bay, but they fell because of the seductress and the seducer (sinner). Even if the seductress is a fellow believer, that is a sinner, and the Bible tells us we should have no fellowship with them. Let it be known that fellowship in this sense does not mean no interaction, it means befriending. How can two walk together except they agree? Evaluate your contact list. Is there anyone you need to let go?

Prayer

Lord let your word light my feet so I will be a bearer of your Good News. Help me to condition my mind and body that I will not sin against you; but bring honor through my surrender and sacrifice in obedience. Amen

Be encouraged...

They word is a lamp unto my feet and a light unto my path. My way is lit.

DAY 29

*"LOSE THE WEIGHT"

Heb 12:1

As believers our race is a matter of life and

death. As a result, quitting is not an option and fitness is a must! It is imperative that we lose weight in order to win the race; but to do this we cannot do a one-off endurance run, we must form new habits which we will engage daily.

❖ **The Race**

Let us understand this race and the need to be fit. It is really a match-up against satanic gladiators, warriors from their youth with THOUSANDS of years of experience.
Therefore, when we prepare, we need to go with

the FORCEFUL attitude, "this means war!" Like David facing Goliath, we must say, 'you come to me with a sword and with a spear, but I come to you IN THE NAME OF THE LORD!' Consider the Roman coliseums where both trained and untrained were put on show whether for sport, punishment, a public spectacle, or entertainment. For the Christian it was a case of kill or be killed, bear the shame, endure the pain, and not give up. On the track, which resembled a typical decathlon event; there were surmounting obstacles, beating opponents, and surviving the brutal challenges with the prize being coming out alive. By nature, the Christian race requires death and the prize eternal life. We are armed by the blood of Jesus and the sword of the Spirit which is the Word of God; with the whole armor, to fight to the death – no retreat, no surrender – enduring to the end until we receive that eternal life; that is the only end we will accept. So, we run.

❖ The Combat Position

With the awareness of who our opponent is, one strategy we should apply in this race is that of law enforcement. A common strategy, especially for hostile or volatile perpetrators is to get them on the ground and neutralize or take control from them, that is to kneel or stand in their neck. Although it seems cruel and perhaps inhumane, it is tactical both for safety and security. When you stand, kneel or add pressure to the neck of the person on the ground, done correctly, the person does not suffocate, it restricts breathing by forcing the person's body to relax. Quit resisting and conform to the power of the one who is in control…that is why we FIGHT from ABOVE. God declared that this was the winning tactical stance of the seed of the woman; "you will bruise (crush) the serpent's head. That is why we stand or kneel in his neck so the satanic gladiator will YIELD to the ONE who is in control.

Rise up you mighty son, anointed daughter, stand up, take your place. The race that is before you might seem daunting; the obstacles that you face, the threats and otherwise prevailing aggressor who seems to be more muscular than you are, but unlike the aggressor you have come into the fight with the winning ticket. The race is fixed in your favor all you need to do to win is fight under His command. So, FIGHT! So, RUN! Run, you are going to win!

❖ How do we win?

We win when we run in an armor that we have proven. It is farcical to believe that you can win a race if you are wearing an armor that you have not tried. The truth is, in this race, in this worldly coliseum, where the rules keep changing and the devil keeps upping the ante you must be dressed right or be left behind; this brutal fight demands that you are fully secured. Even today, as soldiers remain in readiness for deployment, they must complete regular fitness, endurance run and a battle fitness test . The battle (combat) fitness test requires the soldier to don full combat gear and a minimum of a 30-pound filled rucksack and run depending on the military outfit (unit) 880 yard (2 laps around a ¼ mile track) or a 2-mile run or any other variations of that depending on the unit. This test is done because on the battlefield you move, you fight with your equipment, sometimes in trenches, but often on the go. Put your armor on and lose the excess; the sin which easily holds us back. What area of weakness has the devil used to entice you? Are you lonely? Confused? Isolated? Enticed? Distracted? Do not lie or sit there. Stand.

Stand. Gird your waist with truth. Is your waist trustworthy? Are you weak in the hips? Can you be trusted "after dark?" Guard your heart by righteous behavior. The heart is the seat of the emotions and fuel of the will. It influences your behavior. Who has your heart? Put on shoes of peace. Peace prepares the way for the presence of God. 'You will keep him in perfect peace whose mind is stayed on thee' Isaiah 26:3. 'Take the shield of faith.' 'Whose report do you believe?' 'What are you believing God to do in this fight?' 'Do you trust your God?' Trust neutralizes anxiety, fear and doubt and quenches the fiery darts of the enemy. Guard your mind with salvation. Jesus saves! Take the sword of the Spirit, handle God's word skillfully. Wield it with confidence, it is quick and powerful, sharper than a two-edged sword, piercing to the dividing asunder of soul and spirit joints and marrow and is a discerner of the thoughts and intents of the heart. Pray in the Spirit. When we pray in the Spirit we inaugurate or activate the kingdom of God in our life and circumstance. Thy kingdom come. Thy will be done.

Prayer

Dear Lord, I want to win, but my weight is keeping me back. Father, help me to practice the spiritual disciplines that will lead to my spiritual goals and teach me how to wear the armor and dig my heels in for the fight. Amen.

Be encouraged…

Lose the weight, maintain a diet in the Word and exercise in the whole armor of God.

DAY 30

*"YOU HAVE A CROWD"

Heb 12:1

Hebrew 12:1 helps us see the arena, and the coliseum, even more closely.

> 12 Therefore we also, since we are surrounded by so great a cloud of witnesses, let us lay aside every weight, and the sin which so easily ensnares us, and let us run with endurance the race that is set before us, 2 looking unto Jesus, the [a]author and [b]finisher of our faith, who for the joy that was set before Him endured the cross, despising the shame, and has sat down at the right hand of the throne of God.

In the Roman Coliseums hundreds and thousands would gather to witness the ferocious matches that took place between the best gladiators but especially when they were fighting against an "underdog" who was usually a criminal, a Christian or someone captured and made to fight in the tournament as punishment... The underdog would be cruelly beaten, maimed and even killed to the delight of the whirring crowd. As the arena or coliseum was packed to capacity with spectators watching the gruesome tournament, we too have an arena or a coliseum, "a great cloud of witnesses' ' cheering us on. The truth is not every spectator in the coliseums went for the entertainment and "the sport", some went to pray for the Christian brother or sister who was thrown into the fight, while some went to watch their uncle, brother or father make their last stand and others to see the strategies that the victor employed. Just remember as you stand in the fight, the generation behind you is depending on you.

136

❖ **Pre-briefing for the arena**

A. The enemy uses military (war) principles in his fight against us so we must understand his strategies:

B. He exaggerates the features and prowess of the opponent to throw us off (warping)- he makes the opponent look bigger than, smaller than, fewer than, or even more than they really are (David vs Goliath/ new day 100m vs roman gladiators), the art of misdirection is a strategy of the enemy. He will help you find justification for that ungodly alliance and tell you why going to "that place" or doing "that thing" is ok...

C. Putting us on the defensive - subtly offering an armor that will throw us down or the use of threats and insults to weigh us down.

D. Distract us with things and treats. Therefore, to be successful in this gladiator match up we must use SURVIVAL SKILLS. To recap:

- Condition your mind before your body. Let this mind be in you which was also in Christ Jesus. When your mind is conditioned, your body will fall in line.

- Condition your body through fasting and prayer. Forsake or resist the lure of sin and the sinner. Fight or stand. Lean not to your own understanding or power. When we lean on our own understanding, we put more effort in 12 steps and 5 principles than 12 hours of prayer and 5 points of service. Lose the weight.

- Prayer and the Word. When we pray and chant the Word of God into the atmosphere; we are casting down imaginations and every high thing that exalts itself against the knowledge of God. In other words, real power is the power of knowledge, but the power of God is activated through prayer. Let us activate His power. Not by will (desire and determination) not by power, inner might or strength but by the Spirit of the Lord.

As we engage the satanic-gladiator we MUST MATCH the thousands of years, notice, there is a phenomenal wealth of experience with the enemy, do not downplay or underestimate it; even the chiefest of God's angels dare not bring a railing accusation against the prince of the power of the air, instead he said - The Lord rebuke you). We therefore must seek to fight from a strategically higher position of greater power and greater knowledge, of which the scripture says, GREATER IS HE THAT IS IN YOU THAT HE THAT IS IN THE WORLD. One important military strategy that is as old as war is Taking the higher ground. Sun Tzu, a Chinese military legend on whose principles the art of war is grounded, says, 'the general who takes the higher ground takes the war, in other words, fight from above. Perhaps Sun Tzu had spiritual insight, because the Bible tells us that God has raised us UP and caused us to sit together IN HEAVENLY PLACES in Christ Jesus.

Prayer

Lord, lift me up and let me stand, by faith on heaven's table land a higher plain than I have found, Lord plant my feet on higher ground. Amen

Be encouraged...

We stand tall when we fall on our knees...

DAY 31

A LITTLE EXTRA

BE AWARE OF GOD'S PRESENCE

Psalms 139: 7-12
David said in Psalms 139: 7-12

"Where could I go to escape from your Spirit or from your sight? If I were to climb up to the highest heavens, you would be there. If I were to dig down to the world of the dead, you would also be there. Suppose I had wings like the dawning day and flew across the ocean. Even then your powerful arm would guide and protect me. Or suppose I said, "I'll hide in the dark until night comes to cover me over." 12 But you see in the dark because daylight and dark are all the same to you."

God is Omnipresent; He is everywhere. He is outside of us and on the inside. He is outside of time and space, yet He is involved in the intricate details and affairs of our lives; that of our community, country and the world at large. Yes, He is! However, many find the foregone truth difficult to believe probably because they may quickly begin to list the bills they have amassed, the crime and violence within communities, the poverty-stricken countries and the horrendous natural disasters that may have impacted many across the world. As a result, fingers may be pointed at Christians asking, where is your God! Unfortunately, at times we as Christians find ourselves pointing to God, and asking, where are you? "If you were here...", which reminds me of Mary and Martha when their brother Lazarus died. Martha said "Lord, if you were here our brother would not have died." Sometimes it seems lonely, almost as though God has withdrawn himself and has left us to wander through the wilderness, the desert, and the valley alone. As you read this, your thoughts may have revisited the experience when you thought you were alone, and God had gone quiet leaving you to stand all by yourself.

Let us be reminded that the scriptures teach us that we will always have challenges in life. Through great tribulation we will enter the Kingdom of God. Therefore, we must not ignore the fact that the package life presents us is not one of only happiness, prosperity and success but hard knocks as well.

So many of us can relate to the story of the three Hebrew boys; they were forcefully tossed into a fiery furnace; or Daniel's situation, all he did was good. He prayed to His God, yet due to jealousy, he was blackmailed and thrown in the lion's den. We see also that Tamar was raped by her half-brother. It could be a Hannah situation, a woman wanting a child but due to reasons beyond her control, she is unable to give birth. It could also be a Jacob and Esau situation that stirred family rivalry. What about Joseph? His unique gift brought A story of jealousy in the family, or it could be an Esther situation where the threat on your life and that of your family has pushed you to step outside of your comfort zone and seek God for help.

Yes, life can be cruel. It can be so physically, emotionally, psychologically, or mentally, socially, financially, and relationally difficult. Nevertheless, here goes the other side of the story. We can take comfort knowing this very thing, God is with us and will never leave us nor forsake us. A person outside of Christ cannot fully grasp or comprehend this truth. It stuns spectators as they watch a believer pull through the most disturbing and troubling situation. The world watches as the believer takes on each challenge with joy, gentleness, self-control, peace and asks, 'How is that even possible?' However, the believer can wade through the difficulties because he or she is aware of the Father's presence, and that He is always there.

God is also with You. Yes, at this very moment He is with you. Yes, yes, yes, He is. Ok let us go again. The apostles were thrown in prison; many believers in middle eastern and authoritarian-rule countries have been thrown into prison too. So do not get discouraged, instead, approach the situation like Paul and Silas; they sat in prison, sang hymns, and prayed. What about your church sister or brother's testimony? That of your colleague at work, your school or classmate? Too many witnesses to share that God was with them and carried them through or out of their situations. Therefore, take comfort in knowing this, if you find yourself in a lion's den, fiery furnace, being hated by others for no apparent reasons than jealousy, having little or no food like the widow with her little oil and dough; homeless, or broken by past and present experiences, please remember that God is with you. Whether in the heat of the fire or the overwhelming floods, God is and will always be there.

This awareness of God's presence should only produce strength when you become weak, hope when disturbing and troubling reports come your way, when the relationship or marriage you have invested everything in becomes broken, when your children turn against you or fail to support you in your time of need. When you would have lost a loved one, when you are fired, when you become sick, when you experience repeated disappointments. When it seems as if everything you put your hand to fails. When you are called names…God is with you and like David said, "even then your powerful arm would guide and protect me." Isaiah 61:3 states, "To appoint unto them that mourn in Zion, to give unto them beauty for ashes, the oil of joy for mourning, the garment of praise for the spirit of heaviness; that they might be called trees of righteousness, the planting of the Lord, that he might be glorified."

Prayer

Dear God, thank You for always being with me, even in moments that I cannot understand. Thank you for your strength, hope, joy, and peace. Amen

Be encouraged...

I AM with you.

ABOUT THE AUTHOR

Bishop Ricardo O. Henry, an ordained Pastor, has been serving the Church of God, Cleveland TN in credentialed ministry since 1997.

He received his ministerial training at the United Theological College of the West Indies and completed teacher training certification at the College of Agriculture, Science & Education (CASE), Jamaica.

148

He specializes in youth and church ministry development as well as mental health education.

In the recent past, he served as the National Director for Christian Education and Ministerial Care & Development in the New Testament Church of God (NTCG) in the Cayman Islands and Youth Pastor of the George Town NTCG, Cayman Islands.

He currently resides in the Greater Tampa Bay area in Florida, USA and serves as the Student Pastor at the Land O' Lakes Church of God. He is also the primary presenter of the Podcast Fresh Bread available on various podcast platforms (https://anchor.fm/ricardo-henry)

He is married to Tamara and fathers 3 boys Jordaan, Joshuua, and Juude.

RICARDO O. HENRY